DISCARD

D1483124

WAR AND CONFLICT IN THE MIDDLE EAST™

THE SIX-DAY WAR

MATTHEW BROYLES

THE ROSEN PUBLISHING GROUP, INC., NEW YORK

Published in 2004 by The Rosen Publishing Group, Inc.
29 East 21st Street, New York, NY 10010

Copyright © 2004 by The Rosen Publishing Group, Inc.

First Edition

Library of Congress Cataloging-in-Publication Data

Broyles, Matthew.
The Six-Day War / By Matthew Broyles.
    p. cm. — (War and conflict in the Middle East)
Summary: Examines the history behind the 1967 war between Israel
and its surrounding Arab neighbors, Egypt, Syria, and Jordan, plus
biographical notes on important figures and a look at the effects of
this war.
Includes bibliographical references and index.
ISBN 0-8239-4549-9
1. Israel-Arab War, 1967—Juvenile literature. 2. Arab-Israeli conflict—
Juvenile literature. [1. Israel-Arab War, 1967. 2. Arab-Israeli conflict.]
I. Title. II. Series.
DS127.15.B76 2004
956.04'6—dc21

                                                          2003011674

Manufactured in the United States of America

CONTENTS

INTRODUCTION

It was 7:10 AM on June 5, 1967. One hundred eighty-three sleek Israeli fighter jets glided smoothly through the dusty morning air. They passed over Tel Aviv, Israel, heading out over the Mediterranean Sea. United States and Soviet Union warships in the region detected the aircraft formation. So did the radar stations in neighboring Egypt.

It wasn't an unusual sight, since Israel often flew training missions over the Mediterranean. Neither the Americans, Soviets, nor Egyptians were surprised when the planes performed a routine maneuver. The jets quickly dove below radar range and skimmed only 30 feet (9 meters) above the ocean waves.

What happened next surprised everyone watching and, later, the world. The Israeli fighter jets swept into Egypt from the sea and bombed Egyptian military positions.

That day, and the five days that followed, would become known as the Six-Day War. It would forever change the

region we know as the Middle East, a region that the United States has been deeply involved with ever since. The troubles that caused the Six-Day War, like most Middle Eastern conflicts, go back more than 2,000 years, when neither Christianity nor Islam even existed. It is impossible to explain every event over those centuries that led to the 1967 Six-Day War. This book, however, provides a starting point.

The best place to begin is the Roman Empire's conquest of Jerusalem.

CHAPTER 1

THE ARABS AND THE JEWS

It was 63 BC, less than a century before the birth of Jesus Christ. The second kingdom of the people known as the Jews fell at the tip of a Roman sword. The first Jewish kingdom had lasted for more than 1,000 years. The Jews had become a permanent part of the city called Jerusalem and its surrounding lands, named Palestine. Or so it seemed.

Sold into Slavery

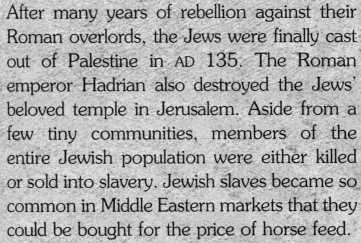

After many years of rebellion against their Roman overlords, the Jews were finally cast out of Palestine in AD 135. The Roman emperor Hadrian also destroyed the Jews' beloved temple in Jerusalem. Aside from a few tiny communities, members of the entire Jewish population were either killed or sold into slavery. Jewish slaves became so common in Middle Eastern markets that they could be bought for the price of horse feed.

Jews who could were allowed to enter Jerusalem once a year to pray at their ruined temple. Otherwise the city was strictly off-limits to its former rulers. Jews began to leave the Middle East for Europe and North Africa. It was a matter of leaving for a better life, or staying and being sold

This 1721 engraving shows the Roman emperor Hadrian's Sant'Angelo Bridge in Rome. It was Hadrian who expelled the Jews from Jerusalem in AD 135. The city would change hands many times before the Jews recaptured its eastern half in 1948, then the western half during the Six-Day War.

into slavery. This began what is known as the Jewish Diaspora, the scattering of the Jews throughout the world that would continue for centuries.

The Coming of Islam

Palestine was not left empty of people. On the contrary, the people now known as Arabs had populated the Middle East for centuries. A large number of them lived in Palestine. In AD 570, the prophet Muhammad was born in Mecca, in what is now Saudi Arabia. He introduced a religion that Arabs and many others would flock to over the centuries to come: Islam. The followers of Islam are known as Muslims.

In AD 638, the Arabs took Jerusalem from the Christians. Christians had ruled the city with an iron fist under the Roman and Byzantine Empires. The Muslim conquerors were far more tolerant of other religions. Jews living in Islamic (formerly Christian) countries, such as Egypt and Spain, were allowed to practice their faith freely. However, the next 400 years would bring only a small number of Jews back to Palestine.

This was just as well because the Christians returned in 1099. The First Crusade was an attempt by Europeans to convert the ancient holy land of Palestine to Christianity. The battle ended up being a bloodbath. The First Crusade took the lives of at least 70,000 Muslims and Jews in Jerusalem alone.

Then in 1187, a Muslim named Saladin led a surprisingly peaceful rebellion against the Christians. The victory

This illustration shows the prophet Muhammad in a cave at Hira in present-day Saudi Arabia. Islam's holy book, the Koran, tells that Muhammad meditated in this cave. The Koran also tells of one of Muhammad's dreams, in which he rises to heaven from the Temple Mount in Jerusalem.

placed control of Palestine back in the hands of Muslims. It would stay this way until 1918. By that time, Palestine had become part of the Turkish Ottoman Empire. Upon the empire's defeat at the end of World War I (1914–1918), the victorious British took control. They drew up arbitrary borders for Palestine, Jordan, and Iraq.

A People Without a Land

Meanwhile, something was happening to change the situation of the Jews of the Diaspora. A wave of anti-Semitism (discrimination against "Semites," as Jews were sometimes called) was sweeping through Europe. It threatened to turn Jews into second-class citizens, as they often had been treated in the past. The hatred against them began to build in the late 1800s. The Jews began to develop a plan to deal with their age-old problem.

This plan was called Zionism. Zionists believed that for Jews to live in peace, they had to have a homeland all their own. Several locations around the globe were considered. Jewish hearts longed for Jerusalem, however. A popular slogan began to circulate: "A people without a land for a land without a people." Except that Palestine already had a people: Arabs.

The British issued the Balfour Declaration in 1917. The declaration proposed that a part of Palestine be established as a national home for the Jews. Half the land would go to the Jews and half to the Arabs. Jerusalem would become an international city, where all religions could worship freely. The Jews agreed to the plan. The Palestinians (the Arabs of

Palestine) flatly refused the proposal. The Jews currently owned only 5 percent of the land and made up less than half of Palestine's population. The Palestinians believed that half was too much to give. What was more, Palestinians were well aware of Zionism. They suspected that if enough Jews came into Palestine, they would claim the entire country as their own.

World War II (1939–1945) brought the Zionist issue to international attention. After the war ended, Adolf Hitler's

Jewish children march in Tel Aviv, Israel, on December 9, 1949, as part of a mass oath of allegiance. The oath was taken at the tomb of Theodor Herzl, the founder of Zionism. The Zionist movement was the primary force behind the 1948 Israeli War of Independence.

horrible slaughter of the Jews became known worldwide. The Allied forces were desperate to find a place where Jews could live free of anti-Semitism. Zionism's rise and the flood of refugees fleeing Nazi Germany had sent thousands of Jews into Palestine. And more were coming.

Birth of a Nation

In 1948, the Palestinians' fear became a reality. Britain withdrew its forces on May 14 without implementing a new government of any kind. A group of Jewish leaders boldly declared the existence of the State of Israel. War began immediately. The Palestinians were helped by larger Arab nations such as Lebanon, Iraq, Syria, Jordan, and Egypt. The armies of these nations attacked Jewish forces and Israel's War of Independence began.

The Jews proved to be stout warriors. They eventually won ownership of Palestine once again—almost. Most of Jerusalem came under Israeli control. The Jordanian army, however, would not be moved from the historic Old City. This was where the temple and the Jews' hearts lay. Before the Israeli army could take control of the Old City, the United Nations imposed a cease-fire order. The battle lines became international borders until further notice.

The home of the Palestinians was now the home of the Jews. The now homeless Palestinian refugees fled Israel by the thousands. Overcrowded and filthy camps sprang up along the new country's borders with Jordan, Lebanon, Syria, and Egypt. The United Nations' attempts to solve the refugee problem failed. Talk of revenge against Israel began to flow among the Palestinian people. This talk spread through the surrounding Arab countries that now sheltered the refugees. Jews were expelled from Arab nations and fled to Israel. This increased the young state's population as well as the tension between Arabs and Jews.

The Jews had never forgotten the loss of their kingdom. And now the Palestinians could not forget the loss of their land. A new war was brewing.

CHAPTER 2

COUNTDOWN TO WAR

On February 28, 1965, a small band of men crossed the Jordanian border into Israel undetected. They placed explosives in a grain silo in the Jewish village of Kfar Hess. The blast ripped a hole in the silo and demolished one of the village's houses. No injuries were reported. The incident caused little concern in Israel. That would soon change. The attack was the first of many to come by a new, shadowy organization known as Fatah.

Terror in Israel

Nearly twenty years had passed since the Israeli War of Independence. The Palestinian refugees were no better off, however, despite endless promises by the Arab nations to fix the problem using peaceful means. Aided and encouraged by Britain and France, Israel had attempted to topple the Egyptian government. The Israelis invaded Egypt during the Suez Crisis in 1956. The crisis created chaos as the refugees fled the battle and the many territories that Israel had captured in the fighting.

These territories included the barren Sinai Peninsula and the Gaza Strip. The Sinai Peninsula is a desert wasteland that separates the African continent from the Middle East.

An Egyptian soldier on patrol in Egypt on November 19, 1956, during the Suez Crisis. Israel, backed by Britain and France, attempted to topple Egypt's president, Gamal Abdel Nasser, resulting in the Suez Crisis, or Suez War.

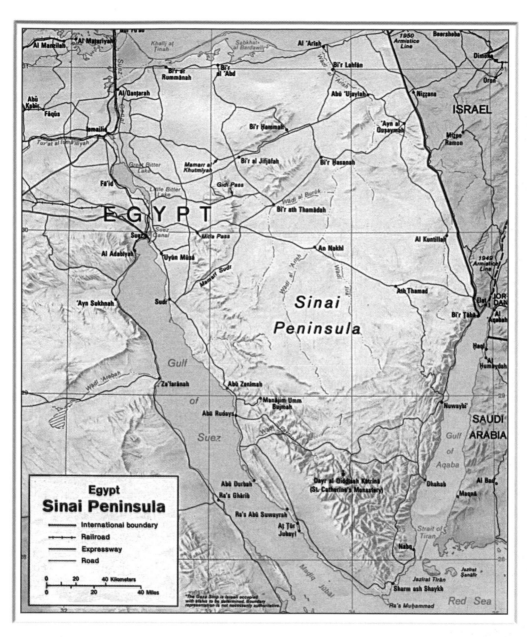

Most of the fighting during the Six-Day War took place on the Sinai Peninsula. The peninsula's importance as a bridge between Africa and the Middle East has made it a crossroads of trade and war since ancient times.

The Gaza Strip is a small section of coastland off the Mediterranean Sea, north of the Sinai. Israel had failed to capture both in the 1948 War of Independence, and thousands of Palestinian refugees had since set up camp in those territories.

When the Egyptian government failed to fall during the Suez Crisis, a cease-fire was put in place. The United Nations insisted that Israel give back all the land it had captured. Israel at first refused. Pressure to withdraw increased from United States president Dwight Eisenhower. Israel backed down and eventually gave the UN what it demanded. A UN peace-keeping force of nearly 9,000 UN troops was sent to Sinai to act as a cushion between Israel and Egypt.

These events meant little to the Palestinians. They had still not gotten any of their land back. In the early 1960s, members of the Fatah group began studying the tactics of resistance movements around the world. They watched how the Algerian rebellion against France succeeded. They also looked closely at how the Viet Cong's assaults on the U.S. troops in Vietnam had confused U.S. military commanders.

A man named Yasser Arafat led Fatah. A former engineer, Arafat seemed a mild-mannered leader. He often used the alias Abu Ammar, which means "the builder." Arafat had visited each Arab capital around the Middle East for nearly ten years. He was trying to get the Arab nations to unite against Israel. Arab leader after Arab leader told him they would try. This unity never happened. Finally, in 1964, Arafat and his Fatah members decided to stop waiting for unity.

The Rise of Nasser

The one man with the diplomatic and military ability to unite the Arab world was Egypt's president, Gamal Abdel Nasser. Nasser came to power when he and a group known as the Free Officers overthrew King Farouk of Egypt in 1952. Soon after, Nasser negotiated Egypt's total independence from British rule. Nasser was a hero and role model to his people and the Arab world. Indeed, for many years, Nasser had promoted Arab unity against America and other Western powers.

Nasser's calls for unity grew louder after the 1956 Suez Crisis. In 1958, he enjoyed intense popularity within the Arab world for standing up to the Israelis. He immediately worked to create the United Arab Republic (UAR). The UAR was an alliance between Syria and Egypt that lasted only until 1961. Constant political differences between the two countries forced Syria's withdrawal from the contract.

Instead, they would attack Israel first. This, they believed, would create the unity the Palestinians desired.

Starting in 1965, Fatah began regular raids into various locations throughout Israel. It grew bolder with each attack. It began to target not only Israeli military personnel, but also civilian targets. The Israeli government was familiar with terrorist tactics. The Israeli army itself had committed deadly raids in the 1940s during Israel's move toward independence. One such bombing happened at the King David Hotel in 1946. That bombing killed ninety-one civilians. Now, fear began to spread among Israelis that the Arab acts of terrorism would grow in number and boldness.

Equally fearful to Israel's leadership was the belief that the Arab nations were behind the Fatah attacks. The raids came across borders from all of Israel's neighboring countries. Yet none of the Arab governments claimed any knowledge of, or responsibility for, Fatah's actions. Nor were they trying to stop these raids. In fact, these countries knew Arafat well. As Fatah's successes grew, its members began to believe that a unified Arab force could bring Israel to its knees.

The Arab World and the Cold War

In truth, anger toward Israel was the only issue that any of the Arab nations could agree on. During the 1950s and 1960s, government-controlled radio in all Arab capitals had waged a war of words. Each nation accused the other of being a U.S. puppet or having secret trade relations with the Israelis.

In Arab capitals, the United States and Israel might as well have been the same country. Both were regarded by Arabs as evil plotters bent on controlling the Middle East. This was in spite of the fact that the United States provided most Middle East nations with weapons. The United States hoped to balance the region to keep war from breaking out. Its belief was that equally powerful nations kept each other in check. Egypt's Gamal Abdel Nasser himself had won power in a coup that was quietly assisted by the United States's Central Intelligence Agency (CIA). Egypt was receiving large amounts of U.S. food aid. The Syrians pointed this out as often as possible.

Yasser Arafat

Yasser Arafat had trained to be a civil engineer. He had also been involved in the Arab-Jewish struggle since his early teens. He smuggled arms to Palestinians before Israel's 1948 War of Independence. He founded Fatah in 1956. Arafat then went on to become head of the Palestine Liberation Organization (PLO) in 1968.

Yasser Arafat at the 1974 Arab Summit conference in Rabat, Morocco.

In 1993, Arafat met in Oslo, Norway, with then–Prime Minister Yitzhak Rabin of Israel. They discussed a peaceful solution to the Arab-Israeli conflict. The Oslo Accords, as the talks became known, did not solve the conflict. They did, however, result in Arafat's election as president of the new Palestinian Council. The council governed the West Bank and the Gaza Strip. Terrorist attacks continued almost constantly for the next ten years. Neither Israel nor the United States believed a peace settlement could be reached with Arafat. In 2003, the United States pressured Arafat into creating the position of Palestinian prime minister. Arafat gave this position to Mahmoud Abbas, the PLO's second in command. His background as a terrorist made the Israeli government uneasy. Abbas resigned his post on September 6, 2003, over control of PLO security forces. He was replaced by Ahmed Qurei, another longtime Arafat associate. Qurei pledged to continue working toward peace with Israel.

The nations of the Middle East were actually pawns in a larger battle in the 1960s: the Cold War. After World War II, the Soviet Union and China had been promoting the spread of Communism throughout the world. They succeeded in places like North Korea, Cuba, and Vietnam. Next on the Soviets' radar were the nations of the Middle East. The United States was deep into its war against Communism in Vietnam. The battle-weary U.S. president Lyndon Johnson didn't need another international battleground to deal with. He hoped that supporting leaders like Nasser and Jordan's King Hussein would keep Communism out of the Middle East. This seemed to be working during the mid-1960s.

Arab leaders, however, suspected they could gain quite a bit more from the U.S.-Soviet chess game. Often, while countries were taking aid from the United States, aid was also arriving from the Soviet Union. Each side was told that it was the favorite. This diplomatic dance was well known to Johnson and to Soviet premier Aleksey Kosygin. Nonetheless, each side continued its arms aid to Arab countries.

Between the late 1950s and the mid-1960s, Arab nations became anxious to prove that they were not puppet regimes of the United States or the Soviet Union. The war of words became more vicious, especially in Syria. Syria began tying itself closer and closer to the Soviets. It hoped this would gain itself military assistance when war at last broke out again with Israel. And war was becoming increasingly likely. By 1966, Israeli forces were launching fierce raids against Syria, Lebanon, and Jordan in retaliation for Fatah's terrorist attacks.

An Israeli tank advances through Syria in June 1967. Syria was the loudest voice for war against the Israelis, and the last to be attacked. Syrian guns pounded Israeli settlements near the Golan Heights throughout the war. The Israeli army finally captured the heights on June 9.

Arab public opinion, always simmering, was inflamed more and more with each Israeli raid. Nasser condemned the raids. But his lack of military action gave the Syrians fuel to chide him. According to Michael Oren's *Six Days of War*, Arab leaders accused Nasser of "selling out Palestine for a few bushels of American wheat." Jordan's prime minister, Wasfi al-Tall, was not to be outdone. Oren states that Tall accused Nasser of "hiding behind UNEF [United Nations Emergency Force] skirts."

Egypt Makes Its Move

As other Arab nations joined in the taunting, Nasser began to realize that his grip on leadership of the Arab world was slipping. Thus, on May 16, 1967, in a move that was against his better judgment, Nasser called for the withdrawal of UNEF forces from the Sinai. At the same time, the Egyptian army began moving its forces closer to the Israeli border. This triggered a similar military buildup by Jordan and Syria in anticipation of war.

Nasser then made a move that would capture not only Israel's attention, but also the world's. He sent troops down to Sharm el-Shaikh, at the tip of the Sinai Peninsula, and blockaded the Straits of Tiran. The Straits of Tiran were the gateway between the Gulf of Aqaba and the markets of the East and Africa. Israel had many ports along the Mediterranean. Its port at Eilat, inside the Gulf of Aqaba, was its only shipping outlet to the Indian Ocean. The straits were also the main channel for Israel's vital oil shipments from Iran.

Soviet Union president Podgorny meets President Nasser of Egypt on June 22, 1967. The meeting took place in Egypt immediately following the Six-Day War. The Soviets replenished Egyptian weaponry after the war, creating an arms buildup which led to the Yom Kippur War in 1973.

By cutting off Israel's eastern port, Nasser demonstrated his commitment to the cause of Arab unity. Nasser's move, however, had also backed Israel into a corner. Israel felt threatened and had to act or face economic ruin. Before this move by Nasser, Israel had not had a single enemy on which to focus retaliation for all of the terrorist attacks. Nasser's move had now given Israel a concrete enemy to defend itself against Fatah. Now Israel had to make a choice.

CHAPTER 3

ISRAEL FACES WAR, AND THE WORLD

Israel had a rough time during 1967. The growing threat of terrorism had brought Jewish immigration to a near halt. World War II reparation payments to Jews from Germany had come to an end. The economy was in trouble. (U.S. monetary aid to Israel was still years away from beginning.) And of course, news that Arab troops were massing on every border did little to boost Israeli morale.

A Nation Challenged

At the center of the storm was Israel's prime minister, Levi Eshkol. Eshkol was a mild-mannered man who wanted to focus on farming, not war. He had taken the reins in 1963 from David Ben-Gurion. Ben-Gurion was a fiery personality who had led the Israeli War of Independence. Eshkol was dedicated to the development of Israel's farms and settlements. He also wanted to build a strong economic foundation for the new state. In the Israeli government, the prime minister doubled as the defense minister. As a result, Eshkol kept his eye closely focused on Nasser's actions.

Eshkol was well aware that the Arabs wanted war. He had supported his chief of staff, Yitzhak Rabin, in building the Israeli

An Israeli vatour bomber flies over Israeli tanks on May 23, 1967, in southern Israel. Israeli prime minister Levi Eshkol ordered the deployment of the Israeli army along the Egyptian border as Egypt's forces gathered in the Sinai.

Yitzhak Rabin

A Jerusalem native, Yitzhak Rabin saw much of the heaviest fighting in Israel's 1948 War of Independence. He later commanded forces in the Suez Crisis and then the Six-Day War. He served as Israel's prime minister from 1974 to 1977 and was elected to the post again in 1992.

In 1993, Rabin met with Yasser Arafat in a historic conference. They negotiated the Oslo Accords, which were meant to lay the groundwork for peace in Israel. In 1994, Arafat, Rabin, and Israeli foreign minister Shimon Peres won the Nobel Peace Prize for the Oslo Accords.

An Israeli law student who disagreed with Rabin's peaceful policies toward the Palestinians assassinated him in 1995. Jordan's King Hussein, U.S. president Bill Clinton, and Egyptian president Hosni Mubarak attended Rabin's funeral. They all praised him as a martyr for peace.

Defense Force (IDF) into a powerful army. As the Arab threat grew, however, concern also grew within the public and inside the government. Many feared that the patient Eshkol might not be up to the job of defending the nation.

One of Eshkol's loudest critics was Ben-Gurion himself. Ben-Gurion even formed a political party to oppose the ruling Mapai Party. He did not support its "wait-and-see" policy toward the Arabs. Many within the Mapai were also beginning to question whether Israel should let the Arabs throw the first stone.

Eshkol had good reason to adopt such a policy. The U.S. government warned that it could not support Israel if it fired the first shot. After the Suez Crisis, the United Nations had

Israeli prime minister Levi Eshkol enters the Knesset (Parliament) building in western Jerusalem in 1966. At that time, Israel only controlled the western part of the city. Eshkol took over the post of prime minister from David Ben-Gurion, who had led the Jews in the 1948 War of Independence.

mostly turned against Israel. Most nations were unlikely to be sympathetic if Israel fired first. The Soviets, in fact, threatened to use military force against any Israeli aggression. U.S. and Soviet naval fleets sat just miles from each other in the Mediterranean Sea. U.S. president Lyndon Johnson feared that any conflict could set off World War III. He offered every possible economic and diplomatic incentive to calm the Israelis' fears of Arab attack.

Moshe Dayan on June 3, 1967, a few days after being sworn in as Israeli defense minister. This was his first press conference after accepting the position. Prior to his appointment, the position of defense minister was part of the job of the prime minister.

Johnson reminded Eshkol of the CIA and UN estimates of military strength in the region. These showed that Israel would win any Arab-Israeli war easily, regardless of who started it. Nonetheless, pressure mounted on Eshkol from his government and the Israeli people. The messages to Washington from Tel Aviv became more and more desperate. Israeli leaders pleaded for a declaration that an attack on Israel would be considered an attack on the United States. This was a declaration that Johnson was not eager to make.

As public confidence in Eshkol dropped, there were calls within the Israeli government and the press for his resignation. Most wanted to bring Ben-Gurion back as prime minister. At last, a compromise was made. Eshkol would remain prime minister. Moshe Dayan, hero of the Suez Crisis, would be given the position of defense minister. The rugged Dayan had lost an eye in World War II and was known for his trademark black eye patch. He immediately began drawing up offensive strategies with Rabin and the IDF.

On the Brink

At the same time, Nasser had committed himself to a first strike. He was confident of both Arab and Soviet backing once the fighting started. By May 27, 1967, Egyptian emotions were high. Nasser's friend and rival Field Marshal 'Abd al-Hakim 'Amer decided to give the order to attack early that morning. This was despite warnings from the Soviets that the United States might take action if Egypt started anything. But forty-five minutes later, 'Amer changed his mind and called

Nasser (seated at left) and 'Amer (seated at right) on May 22, 1967, share a laugh with Egyptian pilots at an air base in the Sinai.

Nasser and 'Amer

The relationship between Gamal Abdel Nasser and 'Abd al-Hakim 'Amer is hard to understand. Nasser and 'Amer were extremely close friends but also political rivals. They had served together in the military and plotted the coup that brought Nasser to power. Their families had even come closer through marriage. Their summer homes stood next to each other. The two men even called each other *akhi* (brother).

Yet the political rivalry between these two powerful men affected every move Nasser made during his presidency. Despite their friendship, 'Amer constantly sought more power within the government. The Soviets considered him an equal to Nasser, a man who fought to keep Egyptian officials under his control.

The Six-Day War destroyed the relationship between Nasser and 'Amer. Immediately after the war, Nasser had 'Amer arrested for planning a coup against him. 'Amer died after a long interrogation in an Egyptian prison, and Nasser grieved for many years.

off the attack. The order to cancel was given just minutes before the air force was scheduled to launch its offensive.

They would not get another chance to strike first.

Fears of a successful Arab first strike weighed heavily on Levi Eshkol. On Saturday, June 3, he sat in his home, awaiting a visit from Israeli diplomats who had just returned from Washington. Oren, again writing in *Six Days of War*, quoted Eshkol worrying aloud to his wife, Miriam: "It's important that the world knows that we waited long enough. I'm sure that we'll win, but it will be a costly war. How long will they let us fight? If it goes well for us, the Russians [Soviets] will surely put the pressure on, and [French president Charles] de Gaulle and others will demand a cease-fire." But the news from Washington was the same: Wait and see.

Finally, on Sunday, June 4, Eshkol and the Israeli cabinet gathered to make the decision. By a vote of 12 to 2, the cabinet decided that Israel would go to war. The attack was scheduled for 7:00 AM the next morning. History was about to be made.

CHAPTER 4

WAR BEGINS

At 8:15 AM in Egypt, on Monday, June 5, nearly every Egyptian air force pilot was eating breakfast. The air force had flown its usual dawn patrol. Since air attacks usually began at sunrise, they had already returned to base, seeing no danger. In fact, there were fewer planes in the air than usual. Airspace had been cleared for a transport plane. This plane was delivering 'Amer and several Egyptian, Iraqi, and Soviet officials to inspect a Sinai air base.

There was only one person in the Arab world who knew something was about to happen. He was the officer on duty at Jordan's 'Ajlun radar facility. 'Ajlun was one of the most sophisticated radar units in the Middle East. At 8:15, the station's screens suddenly lit up with blips. The blips represented Israeli aircraft heading out to sea. Though the number of planes was not unusual, their formation and tight concentration alarmed the officer. He radioed Jordanian headquarters in Amman with the code word for war: *Inab* (which means "grape").

Jordanian general 'Abd al-Mun'im Riyad quickly transmitted the message to Egyptian defense minister Shams Badran in Cairo. Unfortunately, the Egyptians had changed their code frequencies the previous

A burnt out Egyptian aircraft at El Auth airport in the Sinai during the Six-Day War. Runways had been destroyed on June 5, 1967, by an Israeli surprise attack, preventing Egyptian aircraft from taking off. No Egyptian airfields were left operational.

day and had neglected to inform the Jordanians. The warning went unheard.

Shock and Awe

At 8:30 AM, the Israeli air force came screaming out of the clear morning sky. Fighters dove toward Egyptian airfields. They dropped hundreds of 180-pound (82-kilogram) bombs to destroy runways and keep Egyptian jets from taking off. Stunned Egyptian pilots rushed out to their fighters. They found that the Israelis were now targeting the grounded planes. Egyptian fighter jets exploded in deadly fireballs all around them.

The attacks took place simultaneously at airfields throughout Egypt and the Sinai. The Israeli attackers destroyed entire squadrons of fighters and immense Topolov-16 bombers. The bombers' ten-ton payloads exploded into the air. One explosion was so powerful that one of the Israeli jets was blown to pieces as it passed overhead. Before the Egyptian pilots even had time to evacuate the airfields, the next wave of Israeli fighters pounced. They strafed (fired bullets at close range) the runways and set more planes ablaze while killing scores of fleeing pilots and crew.

As the attack raged, there was no response from Egyptian anti-aircraft batteries. The reason was simple and unfortunate: They had been given no-fire orders because 'Amer's transport plane was still en route to Sinai. The Egyptian defense commander feared that the batteries would mistake 'Amer's plane for an attacking Israeli jet.

'Amer's transport plane suddenly found itself with nowhere to land. Israeli fighters swooped all around. The transport craft circled the Sinai for an hour and a half seeking a runway that was not already in flames. It found none. The plane eventually had to land at Cairo's International Airport. 'Amer, lacking military transportation, was forced to take a taxicab to Supreme Headquarters.

By 11:00 AM, Egypt had lost 286 of its 420 military aircraft. Israel's losses stood at 9 planes. Upon attacking an Israeli airfield less than an hour later, the Jordanian air force met a similar fate. Syria followed shortly with its own attack near several northern Israeli positions. The result was another Israeli victory: Israeli fighter pilots destroyed the majority of Syrian aircraft. Israeli general Ezer Weizman telephoned his wife to tell her that the Egyptian air force had been destroyed. According to Donald Neff's *Warriors for Jerusalem*, she replied, "Ezer, are you crazy? At ten o'clock in the morning? You've gone and finished the war?"

Red Sheet over Sinai

Israel's air war was just the beginning of its offensive. At 7:50 AM Israeli time, Egyptian airfields were beginning to burn. Now the Israeli ground forces that had been massing secretly along the Egyptian border received their password to attack: Red Sheet.

The air attack had cut the main Egyptian communication lines. The Egyptian forces in the Sinai had no idea that the war had begun. In fact, Israel's Seventh Armored Brigade was mistaken for a friendly force when it advanced south of Gaza. This illusion didn't last. Suddenly, 124 Israeli Centurion and Patton tanks opened fire. They caught the Egyptians off guard, if only for a moment.

Quickly, Egyptian tanks, artillery, machine guns, and antitank weaponry began pouring their firepower into the advancing tank columns. The Israeli army had penetrated the Sinai at four different points. At each point the fighting was fierce. Casualties were high on both sides, but

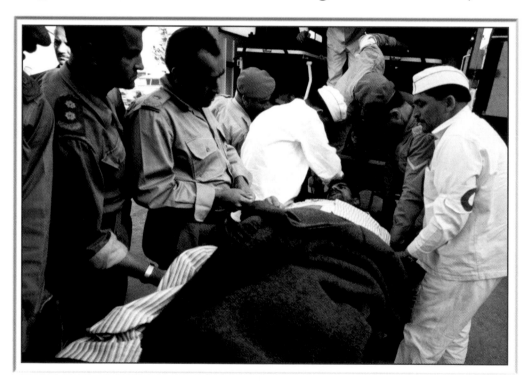

Jordanian medics treat casualties during the Six-Day War. Jordanian losses numbered 700 dead and 6,000 wounded or missing. Jordan's King Hussein was one of the primary Arab voices against the war before public pressure made him join forces with Egypt and Syria.

Israeli progress was steady. They soon broke through the Egyptian lines.

The World Wakes to War

Meanwhile, news of the war spread throughout the world. Lyndon Johnson woke to a ringing phone at 4:35 AM, U.S. eastern standard time (EST). He immediately began working to arrange a cease-fire. Soviet premier Kosygin was no less busy. According to Oren's *Six Days of War*, Kosygin sent Johnson a personal message on the special hot line between Moscow and Washington:

> Kosygin: "It is the duty of all great powers to achieve the immediate cessation of this military conflict. The Soviet government has acted and will act in this direction."

> U.S. secretary of defense Robert McNamara: "What should we say?"

> President Johnson: "My God. What should we say?"

It turned out that neither "great power" was willing to use military force and risk a larger war. Instead, the UN Security Council was called into an emergency session. The debate soon turned as heated as the Sinai battles themselves. Arab delegates charged that the United States and Great Britain had been involved in the air attacks on Egypt. Israeli ambassador Gideon Rafael bluffed, insisting that the Egyptians had fired the first shot. A cease-fire did not seem likely in the near future.

Egypt on the Run

June 5 gave way to June 6, and the second day of the war. The fate of the Egyptian army was looking even less promising. Israel had advanced deep into the Sinai. Egyptian infantry scattered. Destroyed armor and transport vehicles jammed the roads. The Gaza Strip was firmly in Israeli control. Israel was surprised by its quick success and feared a UN-imposed cease-fire. Dayan and Rabin revised war

An Egyptian truck burns in the Gaza Strip on June 5, 1967. This picture was used on the cover of *Time* magazine for its issue immediately following the Six-Day War.

plans, attempting to gain as much ground as possible before the fighting ended.

Back in Cairo, the extent of Egypt's defeat was becoming clear to Nasser and 'Amer. With their air force destroyed and front lines shattered, there was little possibility of turning the tables. The Soviets did not seem anxious to jump in, and the body count continued to rise.

At 5:50 AM on June 6, General Muhammad Fawzi received a message from 'Amer. It advised the garrison at Sharm al-Sheikh to withdraw. It is not known whether Nasser or 'Amer decided to give the order. Later, at 5:00 PM, the order was given for a general retreat from the Sinai.

This was easier said than done, however, as Israeli forces continued to pound Egyptian positions. Plus, Egyptian radio had been broadcasting false reports of victory, which Supreme Headquarters did nothing to contradict. Unit commanders were afraid to tell their troops the truth, when at last it was revealed.

According to Oren, Communications Officer Muhammad Ahmad Khamis remembered: "My soldiers' morale was high, in preparation for the attack—how was I to face them?" Telling them nothing, Khamis ordered his men to drive through the night. "Suddenly, as dawn rose, my driver looked out and saw the [Suez] Canal. 'We have retreated! We have retreated!' he started screaming, weeping with astonishment and fear."

The Sinai was the least of the Arabs' problems now. The city of Jerusalem, holy to the world's three largest religions, was under siege.

CHAPTER 5

JERUSALEM AND THE GOLAN HEIGHTS

King Hussein ibn Talal ibn 'Abdallah of Jordan was in a tight spot. He was generally friendly to the West and not the most warlike of Arab leaders. However, at present, he possessed control of the coveted Old City of Jerusalem. He was faced with the fact that half of Jordan's citizens were Palestinians. In order to stay in power, he had to keep up with the Syrians in their war drive. As a result, Hussein had signed a treaty with Egypt and Syria months earlier. The treaty united the Jordanian and Egyptian military in the event that Israel attacked.

Enemy Neighbors

Unlike Egypt and Syria, however, Jordan's border with Israel was not an open expanse of desert. Many Jordanians in eastern Jerusalem lived, worked, and slept only a few feet from western Jerusalem's Israelis. When the armistice lines were drawn in 1949, the pencil used had even cut through houses. Some buildings were half Jordanian and half Israeli! Opposing military observation posts were only feet apart in many places. On the morning of June 5, the guarded calm that had developed over nearly thirty years seemed intact. Reports of the Sinai offensive blasted

This 1995 picture of Jerusalem shows the border wall set up by the United Nations in 1949 following the Israeli War of Independence. It divides the city into eastern and western halves. Since Jordan's defeat in the Six-Day War, both sides have been under Israeli control.

from Arab radios, but no shots were fired in the Old City or across the Jordanian-Israeli border.

With the majority of Israel's military engaged in the Sinai, the last thing Moshe Dayan wanted was another front. As the morning's attacks began, he sent Hussein a message through UN general Odd Bull in eastern Jerusalem. He promised that Israel would not attack Jordan unless it was attacked first. Hussein knew the Israelis as well as he knew his own people. He had no doubt that war would come to Jerusalem one way or another.

The Battle for Jerusalem

At 9:30 AM, Hussein spoke to his people over the radio. He announced that Jordan had been attacked and that "the hour of revenge had come." Hussein had just gotten off of the phone with Nasser. Nasser assured him that the Israeli army was taking a beating. Hussein ordered Jordanian artillery batteries to open fire on Tel Aviv. Within hours, total war broke out in Jerusalem.

While heavily fortified in the Sinai, Israeli positions in the West Bank were down to skeleton crews. Fighting in Jerusalem was fierce and often hand to hand. The combat wasn't restricted to the military as deadly battles broke out in the city. Civilian Rachel Kaufman and three workers held off Jordanian troops with old Czechoslovakian guns at her husband's farm. Other citizens either found hiding places or took up arms throughout Jerusalem.

Other Jordanians fled Jerusalem across the shallow Jordan River with as many possessions as they could carry. Many of them were Palestinian refugees from Israel's 1948 War of Independence. Israeli reinforcements arrived and the tide began to turn against the Jordanians. It became clear that very soon, Levi Eshkol would have to make another tough decision: Should Israel take the Old City?

The reclaiming of Jerusalem had been the dream of the Jews through nearly 2,000 years of the Diaspora. Now it tempted the Israeli leadership with its closeness. But how would the world react?

The United States had forced Israel to give up its captured territory after the Suez Crisis. Eshkol feared that Israel would not be allowed to keep the Old City after the fighting stopped. U.S. pressure, international law, and the threat of Soviet military force loomed large in Eskol's mind. To win the prize only to return it seemed too heartbreaking to imagine. Neff writes in *Warriors for Jerusalem* that Interior Minister Haim Moshe Shapira voiced his fear aloud: "Should we do it? Do we dare do it?"

Pressure from opposing figures in the government grew. Activist and future prime minister Menachem Begin and Labor Minister Yigal Allon pushed for the Old City's capture. This, combined with the intoxicating dream of a Jewish Jerusalem, soon turned the tide for Eshkol. At last, according to Neff, he declared, "We are going to take the Old City of Jerusalem, in order to remove the danger of the bombardment and the shelling incessantly being carried out by

Jordan." Whatever the reasons, Israel had decided to leave the international debate until another day.

Jordanian resistance proved fierce. The Israeli army pressed forward. On the morning of June 7, 1967, Colonel Mordechai "Motta" Gur led his force into the Old City. Crashing through the Lion's Gate, they rushed immediately to the Temple Mount. To the Jews present, international opinion took second place to the fulfillment of a 2,000-year-old dream. Soldiers chanted at the sacred Western

An Israeli soldier prays at the Western Wall, or "Wailing Wall" in 1967. Jews had not been allowed to visit the wall for the previous twelve years. The wall is all that is left of the temple destroyed by the Romans after they exiled the Jews in AD 135.

"Wailing" Wall, the last remains of the temple. Typical was this proclamation, according to Neff: "I, General Schlomo Goren, chief rabbi of the Israeli Defense Force, have come to this place never to leave again."

Israeli cabinet members and civilians began streaming into the Old City. They gathered at the Western Wall in ecstasy. Eshkol himself visited the wall that afternoon. He slipped a piece of paper with a prayer written by his wife between the stones. As the fighting died down, he met with Christian leaders within the Old City. He promised them that all churches and shrines would be protected. He also promised that all denominations would be allowed to worship freely. This was something the Jordanians had denied Jews for twelve years.

Syria Looms

The Jordanian and Egyptian armies were still making their reluctant yet hasty retreats on June 8. One threat, however, remained for the Israelis: Syria. Syrian guns from the Golan Heights had been shelling northern Israeli settlements since the Sinai campaign had begun. Moshe Dayan continued to turn down northern generals' requests for permission to counterattack. Dayan was concerned enough about the two existing fronts. He worried that the IDF couldn't handle another one. Dayan was particularly concerned since Syria had the closest ties with the Soviet Union. However, events in the UN and in Syria would soon change his mind.

On June 8, at 9:00 PM U.S. EST, Egyptian foreign minister Mahmoud Riad contacted Egypt's UN ambassador,

Muhammad El Kony. El Kony had been reading reports of massive Egyptian victories, invented by Egyptian military commanders. He was preparing a speech to reject yet another cease-fire offer. This time, however, Riad told him the truth about the state of Egypt's forces.

"It cannot be!" El Kony replied. The idea of Israeli victory made no sense alongside the military reports. He suspected an Israeli trick and called Nasser personally, according to Oren. "You did well by calling, Muhammad," Nasser assured him, "but yes, you are to accept the cease-fire."

At 9:35 PM, Oren states, El Kony entered the security council chamber weeping. "I have the honor to convey, upon instructions of my government, the decision to accept the call for a cease-fire," he announced, "provided that the other side ceases firing as well."

There were many within Israel who believed that no cease-fire could be agreed upon yet. The Syrian positions atop the towering Golan Heights were still raining shells on Israeli settlements. Among those targeting Syria was Levi Eskhol. He gathered his advisers around him on the evening of June 8. He hoped to capture at least part of the Golan Heights and remove the threat of future shelling. According to Oren, Yigal Allon agreed: "I prefer the Syrian ridge without [keeping good relations with] the Soviets, to the Syrians remaining on that ridge and our retaining our ties with the Soviets."

Moshe Dayan's supporters were less convinced, states Oren, including Religious Affairs minister Zorach Warhaftig: "I'm no coward," he declared, "but a break with the USSR [the Soviet Union] means breaking with ten other countries . . . it could lead to our expulsion from the UN. We are drunk and not on wine."

News arrived that the Egyptians were ready to accept a cease-fire and that Syrian acceptance would soon follow. The decision was made that no action would be taken on the Syrian front at that time. But Dayan, Rabin, and Eskhol agreed that they might approve a Golan attack if the situation changed.

Soldiers observe the destruction at Syria's Golan Heights following its capture by Israel. The Syrian defeat was the last military action of the Six-Day War. The last Syrian position to be captured was Mount Hermon, which overlooks Syria's capital of Damascus.

One reason for Dayan's restraint was that the bulk of the Israeli army was down in Gaza and Sinai. Most of the remaining troops were now in Jerusalem and the West Bank. A small Israeli force was all that remained in the north. The Golan Heights were heavily fortified on the Syrian side. It was believed that any battle would likely cause huge Israeli casualties.

Last Stand on the Golan Heights

Major Eli Halahmi, who supervised research on the Syrian army, received a new set of aerial photos that night. They showed that the Golan Heights city of Quneitra was now totally undefended. He wasted no time in passing the photos up the chain of command. By the dawn of June 9, Dayan received the photos. According to Oren, Dayan also received an intercepted message from Nasser to Syrian president Nureddin al-Attasi in Damascus: "For your own benefit allow me to advise you to accept the cease-fire immediately ... This is the only way of saving the valiant Syrian army. We have lost this battle."

Dayan scribbled a quick note to Eskhol: "Last night I had no idea that the leadership of Egypt and Syria would crumble like this and give up the battle. In any event, we must exploit this opportunity to the utmost. A great day." Not waiting for a response from Eshkol, he telephoned Northern Command general David "Dado" Elazar, waking him.

Dayan: "Can you attack?"

Elazar: "I can—and right now."

Dayan: "Then attack."

At 9:40 AM on June 9, the Israeli air force unleashed a brutal assault on the Golan Heights. It fired rockets taken from captured Egyptian supplies. While many Syrian positions were undefended, Golan Heights was by no means deserted. The remaining Syrian forces stayed in their bunkers, ready to fight.

And fight they would. The original Israeli attack plan called for a nighttime assault. Soldiers scaling the steep 2,000-foot (610-meter) heights by day would be easy targets for Syrian guns. With a cease-fire looming, however, time was running out. Israeli forces advanced in broad daylight, taking heavy fire from dug-in Syrian tanks. Exhausted Israeli tank brigades recently arrived from the Sinai were called into action. They threw everything they had at the hardened Syrian bunkers. Without critical air support, though, the Syrian positions could not last, and they began to fall one by one.

Arab Unity Stretched

The Syrian government pleaded with Egypt for assistance. This was unlikely to arrive. Reeling from the staggering defeat of his military, Nasser had fallen into a deep depression. Field Marshal 'Amer had gone hysterical, crying and ranting about conspiracies, and threatened to commit suicide. Nasser found him and calmed him down, then made a decision, according to Oren: "A regime which is unable to defend the borders of its homeland loses its legitimacy. As sad as we may be right now, we have to know that our rule has ended in tragedy." At 6:30 PM on Cairo radio, Nasser calmly announced his resignation as president.

The moment those words echoed from radios throughout Egypt, the streets of Cairo suddenly filled with people. So did the streets of nearly every city in the Arab world. Tearing their hair and clothing, the demonstrators cried, "Nasser, don't leave us!" and cried for the president's return. Nasser's photograph filled the screen on Egyptian television. King Hussein later broadcast a message over Radio Amman: "I urge you to respond to the nation's wishes and stay on. The battle is only beginning." Never one to resist public support, Nasser quickly withdrew his resignation, though he accepted 'Amer's.

Meanwhile, news from the Golan Heights had turned the situation in the UN Security Council from bad to worse. A cease-fire was now accepted by the Arab nations. Soviet ambassador Nikolai Federenko demanded that Israel be "severely punished" for its attack. He warned that "non-compliance [with the cease-fire] will have the gravest consequences for the Israeli State."

The United States was also growing impatient with Israel. Scribbling on a notepad during a National Security Council briefing, according to Oren, President Johnson complained, "I had a firm commitment from Eskhol [honoring the cease-fire] and he blew it. That old coot isn't going to pay any attention."

As June 10 dawned, however, the warnings from both Moscow and Washington had become impossible to ignore. The U.S. Sixth Fleet had begun to steam toward Israel's coast. The Soviets had broken off diplomatic relations with

Tel Aviv. Israel rushed to capture as much strategic territory as possible. The last target Yitzhak Rabin authorized was Mount Hermon, which overlooked downtown Damascus.

Finally, at 3:00 PM, Moshe Dayan met with UN general Odd Bull in Tel Aviv. He agreed to a cease-fire, which did indeed go into effect at 6:00 PM. The Six-Day War was over.

The hard work was just beginning.

CHAPTER 6

AFTERMATH

As the diplomatic dust began to settle in the UN, talk of an official resolution continued. The United States and Soviet Union wanted a clear statement from the UN that would prevent any future conflict. Arabs and Israelis were more concerned with the matter of occupied territory. Israel had tripled in size in six days and was not anxious to part with its winnings.

Arab diplomats demanded that Israel withdraw immediately and unconditionally. They argued that the capture of the territories was against international law. Israel wanted rock-solid guarantees that it would not be attacked from those same territories if it gave them back. The battle lines were drawn and were unlikely to move.

UN Resolution 242

In addition, during negotiations Israel would only deal with the Sinai, Gaza, and the Golan Heights. No mention was made of Jerusalem. The United States continued to assure the UN Security Council that it supported Israeli withdrawal. Washington, however, began to discover how limited its influence was when it came to the matter of Jerusalem.

Meanwhile, one issue that had played such a role in starting the war remained unresolved: the plight of the Palestinians.

On June 5, 1967, the United Nations Security Council convened to discuss the outbreak of hostilities in the Middle East.

Near Jerusalem's Temple Mount, 135 Muslim houses were bulldozed to make way for a prayer plaza. Three villages in the West Bank were completely destroyed days after the war. The Israeli soldiers assigned to the demolition refused to carry out the order, but the order was later completed. Refugee camps, already overflowing and badly maintained, were now packed with homeless Palestinians.

However, the UN seemed to be overlooking the Palestinian issue. The debate concentrated more on resolving territorial disputes and avoiding future warfare. On November 22, 1967, UN Resolution 242 passed. The resolution was written in language vague enough to please both sides. It called for an effort to negotiate land for peace, without actually specifying when and how.

Terror Returns to Israel

Even before the UN passed Resolution 242, Israel found that there was one foe left undefeated: Fatah. Starting in October, terrorist attacks once again plagued the country. Only this time, the acts were deadlier and more daring. Despite the passage of Resolution 242, rumors grew of Arab leaders planning a new war. These rumors would prove true in 1973, when Egypt launched the Yom Kippur War.

After passage of Resolution 242, the United States once again focused its attention on Vietnam. But it would never be able to fully detach itself from Middle East politics. Nor would the Soviet Union. In the years to come, the Soviets would continue to supply Arab nations with arms and political support.

The Legacy of War

The Six-Day War did not ease political tension in the Middle East. Instead, it fanned the flames of a conflict that remains unresolved to the present day. Terror attacks continue to threaten Israeli citizens. Palestinians continue to be held in their refugee camps.

Israel returned the Sinai Peninsula to Egypt in 1979. However, Israel continues to occupy the Gaza Strip, the Golan Heights, the West Bank, and Jerusalem. Refugee camps established as long ago as 1949 remain in the Arab world. Negotiations continue between the United States, Israel, and the new Palestinian Authority to resolve the crisis. Islamic terror organizations have moved beyond the small size of Fatah and have become threats to world peace.

The world now moves into a new era of global communication and cooperation. But we continue to feel the effects of those six days in 1967. As of this writing, the United States continues to press for peace in the Middle East, and the world.

anti-Semitism Racist hatred of Jews.

Central Intelligence Agency (CIA) An independent agency of the United States government responsible for collecting and coordinating intelligence and counterintelligence activities abroad in the national interest.

Cold War A state of political tension and military rivalry between nations that stops short of full-scale war. This situation existed between the United States and Soviet Union following World War II and ended in 1989 with the collapse of the Soviet Union.

Communism A system of government in which the state plans and controls the economy and a single party holds power, claiming to make progress toward a higher social order in which all goods are equally shared by the people.

Islam The religion of the Muslims, following the teachings of the prophet Muhammad and the scriptures of the Koran.

Judaism The religion of the Jews, tracing its origins to Abraham and having its spiritual and ethical principles based in the Hebrew scriptures of the Old Testament and the Talmud.

martyr One who has been killed because of his or her religious or political principles.

Nobel Peace Prize The prize awarded annually by the Nobel Foundation for outstanding achievements in the promotion of world peace.

Ottoman Empire A vast Turkish nation of southwestern Asia, northeastern Africa, and southeastern Europe. It was founded in the thirteenth century by Osman I and ruled by his descendants until after World War I.

Palestine Liberation Organization Coordinating council for Palestinian organizations, founded in 1964 at the first Arab summit meeting.

Roman Empire An empire that succeeded the Roman Republic during the time of Augustus, who ruled from 27 BC to AD 14. The last emperor, Romulus Augustulus (born c. AD 461), was deposed by Goths in 476, the traditionally recorded date for the end of the empire.

Soviet Union A former Communist country in eastern Europe and northern Asia; established in 1922; included Russia and fourteen other Soviet Socialist republics (Ukraine, Belarus, and others); officially dissolved on December 31, 1991.

Viet Cong A Vietnamese person belonging to or supporting the National Liberation Front of the nation formerly named South Vietnam.

Vietnam War A long military conflict (1954–1975) between the Communist forces of North Vietnam supported by China and the Soviet Union, and the non-Communist forces of South Vietnam supported by the United States.

United Nations (UN) An international organization composed of most of the countries of the world. It was founded in 1945 to promote peace, security, and economic development.

Zionism A Jewish movement that arose in the late nineteenth century in response to growing anti-Semitism and sought to reestablish a Jewish homeland in Palestine. Modern Zionism is concerned with the support and development of the State of Israel.

Organizations

Council on American-Islamic Relations (CAIR)
453 New Jersey Avenue, SE
Washington, D.C. 20003
(202) 488-8787
Web site: http://www.cair-net.org

Center for Jewish History
15 West 16th Street
New York, NY 10011
(212) 294-8301
Web site: http://www.cjh.org

The Jewish-Arab Center for Peace
Givat Haviva
M.P. Menashe 37850
Israel
e-mail: givat_il@inter.net.il
Web site: http://www.inter.net.il/~givat_h/givat/arabcent.htm

Web Sites

Due to the changing nature of Internet links, the Rosen Publishing Group, Inc., has developed an online list of Web sites related to the subjects of this book. This site is updated regularly. Please use this link to access the list:

http://www.rosenlinks.com/wcme/sidw

Harris, Nathaniel. *Israel and the Arab Nations in Conflict*. Austin, TX: Raintree/Steck-Vaughn, 1999.

Kort, Michael. *The Handbook of the Middle East*. Brookfield, CT: Twenty-First Century Books, 2002.

Long, Cathryn J. *The Middle East In Search of Peace*. Brookfield, CT: Millbrook Press, 1996.

McAleavy, Tony. *The Arab-Israeli Conflict*. New York: SIGS Books and Multimedia, 1998.

Ross, Stewart. *Causes and Consequences of the Arab-Israeli Conflict*. Austin, TX: Raintree/Steck-Vaughn, 1996.

Schroeter, Daniel J. *Israel: An Illustrated History*. New York: Oxford University Press, 1998.

Waldman, Neil. *The Golden City: Jerusalem's 3000 Years*. Honesdale, PA: Boyds Mill Press, 2000.

Williams, Colleen Madonna Flood. *Yasir Arafat*. Philadelphia: Chelsea House Publishers, 2002.

ABCNews.com. "Newsmakers: Ariel Sharon."
Retrieved May 6, 2003 (http://abcnews.go.com/
reference/bios/asharon.html).

ABCNews.com. "Newsmakers: Yasser Arafat." Retrieved
May 6, 2003 (http://www.abcnews.go.com/
reference/bios/arafat.html).

CNN.com. "'Soldier for Peace' Rabin Buried."
Retrieved May 6, 2003 (http://www.cnn.com/
WORLD/9511/rabin/funeral/wrap/index.html).

Infoplease.com. "Yitzhak Rabin." Retrieved May 6,
2003 (http://www.infoplease.com/ce6/people/
A0840880.html).

Neff, Donald. *Warriors for Jerusalem: The Six Days
That Changed the Middle East*. New York:
Linden Press/Simon & Schuster, 1984.

North Park University WebChron. "The Yom Kippur
War, 1973." Retrieved May 6, 2003
(http://campus.northpark.edu/history/WebChron/
MiddleEast/YomKippurWar.html)

Oren, Michael B. *Six Days of War: June 1967 and
the Making of the Modern Middle East*. New
York: Oxford University Press, 2002.

The Peace Encyclopedia. "The War of Independence,
1948." Retrieved May 6, 2003
(http://www.yahoodi.com/peace/warindep.html).

INDEX

INDEX

About the Author

Matthew Broyles is a writer and musician living in New York City.

Photo Credits

Cover, pp. 1, 3, 4–5 © Vittoriano Rastelli/Corbis; pp. 6–7 © Historical Picture Archive/Corbis; pp. 9, 11, 29, 30 © Bettmann/Corbis; p. 6 © Historal Picture Archive/Corbis; p. 14–15, 20, 24, 34–35, 54–55 © Hulton/Archive/Getty Images; p. 16 © Perry-Castãnedia Library Map Collection/The University of Texas at Austin; p. 22 © Corbis; pp. 26–27, 32 © AP/World Wide Photos; p. 38 © Tim Page/Corbis; pp. 40, 46, 49 © David Rubinger/Corbis; p. 42–43 © Annie Griffiths Belt/Corbis.

Designer: Nelson Sá; **Editor:** Mark Beyer;
Photo Researcher: Nelson Sá